Endorsements fo

"Christians are pı
does Scripture struc̗u̗r̗e̗ a̗ c̗h̗u̗r̗c̗h̗, order worship, or-
ganize ministry, and define biblical leadership? Those
are just examples of the questions that are answered
clearly, carefully, and winsomely in this new series from
9Marks. I am so thankful for this ministry and for its
incredibly healthy and hopeful influence in so many
faithful churches. I eagerly commend this series."

R. Albert Mohler Jr., President, The Southern
Baptist Theological Seminary

"Sincere questions deserve thoughtful answers. If you're
not sure where to start in answering these questions, let
this series serve as a diving board into the pool. These
mini-books are winsomely to-the-point and great to
read together with one friend or one hundred friends."

Gloria Furman, author, *Missional Motherhood*
and *The Pastor's Wife*

"As a pastor, I get asked lots of questions. I'm approached by unbelievers seeking to understand the gospel, new believers unsure about next steps, and maturing believers wanting help answering questions from their Christian family, friends, neighbors, or coworkers. It's in these moments that I wish I had a book to give them that was brief, answered their questions, and pointed them in the right direction for further study. Church Questions is a series that provides just that. Each booklet tackles one question in a biblical, brief, and practical manner. The series may be called Church Questions, but it could be called 'Church Answers.' I intend to pick these up by the dozens and give them away regularly. You should too."

Juan R. Sanchez, Senior Pastor, High Pointe Baptist Church, Austin, Texas

What If I Don't Feel Like Going to Church?

Church Questions

What If I Don't Feel Like Going to Church?

Gunner Gundersen

:: CROSSWAY®

WHEATON, ILLINOIS

Trade paperback ISBN: 978-1-4335-6889-3
ePub ISBN: 978-1-4335-6892-3
PDF ISBN: 978-1-4335-6890-9
Mobipocket ISBN: 978-1-4335-6891-6

Library of Congress Cataloging-in-Publication Data

Names: Gundersen, David, author.
Title: What if I don't feel like going to church? / David 'Gunner' Gundersen.
Description: Wheaton, Illinois : Crossway, 2020. | Series: Church questions | Includes index.
Identifiers: LCCN 2019050328 (print) | LCCN 2019050329 (ebook) | ISBN 9781433568893 (trade paperback) | ISBN 9781433568909 (pdf) | ISBN 9781433568916 (mobi) | ISBN 9781433568923 (epub)
Subjects: LCSH: Church attendance.
Classification: LCC BV4523 .G86 2020 (print) | LCC BV4523 (ebook) | DDC 254.5—dc23
LC record available at https://lccn.loc.gov/2019050328
LC ebook record available at https://lccn.loc.gov/2019050329

Crossway is a publishing ministry of Good News Publishers.

BP			29	28	27	26	25	24	23	22	21	20
15	14	13	12	11	10	9	8	7	6	5	4	3	2	1

And all who believed were together . . .

Acts 2:44

The most important time to be at church is when you don't feel like it.

I once talked with three Christians in a week—two struggling with depression, and a third going through a tough breakup—who'd stopped gathering with God's people. Whether for weeks or months, all three stopped showing up on Sundays.

One said it would be unsatisfying because there wasn't a sense of connection. Another said it would be awkward because he didn't want to see his ex. The other said it would be unhelpful because she had no desire to be there anymore.[1]

I'm not here to minimize their burdens or condemn them for feeling the way they did. I'm not writing to them or about them. I'm simply writing to every Christian who feels the way they felt, who feels (as I have felt before) like gathering with God's people will be unsatisfying, unhelpful, or just plain awkward.

I'm writing to say something I said to all three of my friends: the most important time to be at church is when you don't feel like it.

My goal is simple: I want to motivate Christians to meet together with consistency, joy, and purpose. I'm writing to Christians who love Jesus and want to follow him but who struggle to understand, appreciate, or make time for the church.

What's in a Feeling?

Feelings can be complicated. We all know we shouldn't blindly follow them. Yet our feelings can reveal what we really like, want, or think. Since this book is about how we *feel* about going to church, here are three things to remember about our feelings.

First, *our feelings shouldn't dictate our choices.* If we always followed our feelings, no marriage would survive, kids would only eat candy, and marathons wouldn't be a thing. Preachers who didn't feel ready on Saturday night wouldn't show up on Sunday morning, Christians under persecution would just stay home, and every believer who's unhappy with someone else at church would hold a grudge instead of holding the door. Yet we know we shouldn't do whatever we feel or avoid whatever's uncomfortable. Scripture reminds us, "There is a way that seems right to a man, but its end is the way to death" (Prov. 14:12).

Instead, we recognize that *our core desires run deeper than our emotions.* A frustrated mom might feel like collapsing into a well-deserved nap, but instead she keeps watching her three young kids. Why? Because she wants them protected more than she wants her rest. In the same way, every true Christian has a new heart for God and his people that keeps perking up and pushing us forward even when we're weary (Heb. 8:10–11). Our desires are layered, and our deepest desires often contradict our passing emotions.

At the same time, *most feelings are symptoms of underlying causes.* When we don't feel like going to church, something deeper may be going on—not always but often. As Scripture says, "The purpose in a man's heart is like deep water" (Prov. 20:5). Therefore, laying ourselves on the operating table and letting God's Spirit open us through his word is the safest treatment for our souls. "For the word of God is living and active, sharper than any two-edged sword, piercing to the division of soul and of spirit, of joints and of marrow, and discerning the thoughts and intentions of the heart" (Heb. 4:12).

Diagnosing the Heart

There are many reasons Christians might not feel like going to church. But if you can discern the reason behind your reluctance, the path forward becomes clearer. An accurate diagnosis is half the cure—even when the remedy is hard to apply. So what are some reasons attending church might be a struggle?

Physical Reasons

Some Christians struggle to attend church for *physical* reasons like exhaustion, illness, disease, or chronic pain. It might be obvious or unnoticed, temporary or permanent, diagnosed or mysterious. Regardless, you're physically burdened. The world is broken, you're not a machine, and sometimes the spirit is willing but the flesh is weak (Matt. 26:41).

Spiritual Reasons

Maybe the dominant reason is *spiritual*. You're in a dark place, Christianity has lost its luster, or you're living in hidden sin. Maybe feasting on the world has sapped your spiritual appetite, or you're going through your first dry season as a Christian. Perhaps you resonate with the psalmist: "Why are you cast down, O my soul, and why are you in turmoil within me?" (Ps. 42:5).

Relational Reasons

Sometimes the challenge is *relational*— a marital problem, a broken friendship, an awkward personality. Maybe you're single or widowed, and you feel out of place around all the families. Maybe you've disagreed with a leader, and there's lasting tension. Maybe you've been judged or rebuked by someone, and seeing them triggers anger and shame. Maybe you'll be disowned or lose credibility if you identify with the Christian faith. Regardless, Psalm 133:1 is far from your experience: "Behold, how good and pleasant it is when brothers dwell in unity!"

Logistical Reasons

Maybe your issues are mainly *logistical*. You live far away, or your work hours change from week to week. Perhaps you're often traveling, or the weekends offer valuable time to catch up on homework or house projects. For many moms, hauling young children to church can be chaotic and exhausting, and arguing with older kids each week can leave you feeling like a hostage negotiator. Whatever the situation, getting to and from church is challenging.

Preferential Reasons

Some frustrations are about *preferences*. You don't like the music, the liturgy, the way people dress, or the leadership style. You wish the sermon were shorter, the people friendlier, the coffee better. Your preferences might reflect biblical principles or might just be nitpicky. But whether you're right or wrong, constant frustration isn't a good sign.

Cultural Reasons

Some of our preferences are *cultural*. You might be a blue-collar guy at a white-collar church, or a racial minority in a church where few understand your experience. You might be an immigrant, an overseas worker, or a third-culture kid. Whether it's a language barrier or other elements that keep you feeling like an outsider, cultural differences can make it difficult to engage at church.

Recreational Reasons

Some people struggle with church for *recreational* reasons. The weekends are prime time for hobbies, adventures, tournaments, travel, or kids' sports programs. With a busy week behind you and fresh opportunities before you, it can be hard to prioritize church.

Missional Reasons

Sometimes Christians have a hard time with church because there's little *direction* coming from the leaders. We want to participate, contribute, and give ourselves to the mission Christ gave his disciples (Matt. 28:18–20). But a lack of leadership leaves you feeling like your church is on the sidelines instead of the frontlines.

Doctrinal Reasons

Sometimes Christians can't find a church that aligns with their *beliefs*. The church you attend might be your default church but not your desired church, so you feel doctrinally homeless. You'd love for your church to line up with your convictions, but you don't want to be divisive. Your differences might be hindering you from connecting or serving, and you might find yourself on the margins or on the verge of leaving.

Intellectual Reasons

Other Christians find church difficult for *intellectual* reasons. The messages seem trite and cliché, and you leave Sunday with none of your objections answered. Grad school, an intellectual occupation, diverse friendships, or a deep background in other religions makes you long for deeper thinking. Or maybe you're just a contrarian, and you're always playing devil's advocate. You're committed to Christ, but your church isn't a place you would bring a non-believing friend.

Transitional Reasons

There are also *transitional* challenges to navigate. Sometimes these transitions are personal—you're stepping away from a ministry or moving to a new city or searching for a new church. Other times the church itself is transitioning. A young new pastor takes the helm. Close friends leave. The church moves locations. Even a needed season of change can go on for too long and become a marathon without a finish line.

Personal Reasons

Finally, some have *personal* problems with the church. Maybe you've been abused by "spiritual authorities," witnessed a pastoral scandal, or endured a church split. In some situations you might bear some responsibility, but even when you're completely innocent, there's still pain. Whether your wounds are caused by others or self-inflicted, personal history can make it hard to love a church, trust a church, or even attend a church.

———

We all have different personalities, situations, and challenges. But I hope the categories above kickstart your thinking as you assess your own situation. You can use the chart "Why I Don't Feel Like Going to Church" to rank and explain the reasons that resonate with you the most.

Why I Don't Feel Like Going to Church		
Rank	Reason	Explanation
	physical	
	spiritual	
	relational	

Why I Don't Feel Like Going to Church		
Rank	*Reason*	*Explanation*
	logistical	
	preferential	
	cultural	
	recreational	
	missional	
	doctrinal	
	intellectual	
	transitional	
	personal	
	other:	

Asking for Help

I can't come through the page, diagnose your problem, and guarantee an easy solution. Often no silver bullet exists for the challenges we face in our churches. But God promises wisdom for those who ask: "If any of you lacks wisdom, let him ask God, who gives generously to all without reproach, and it will be given him" (James 1:5). So where do we find this wisdom to move forward?

The Word of God

The main place to go for wisdom is God's word, praised by the psalmist as "a lamp to my feet and a light to my path" (Ps. 119:105). Scripture comes from the perfect mind of God, and it teaches, corrects, and trains us so that we're "equipped for every good work" (2 Tim. 3:16–17). When the path forward seems rocky or unclear, we're reminded:

> Trust in the LORD with all your heart,
> and do not lean on your own
> understanding.

In all your ways acknowledge him,
> and he will make straight your paths.
>> (Prov. 3:5–6)

Like a stream smoothing a stone, submerging your heart in the truth will shape your habits over time.

Discerning Friends

Proverbs 18:1 says, "Whoever isolates himself seeks his own desire; he breaks out against all sound judgment." When we're struggling with our churches, it's easier to choose frustrated silence over healthy communication. But flying solo is dangerous, because sin is crafty, and like clay in the sun, our hearts are easily hardened (Eph. 4:14; Heb. 3:13).

Instead, Ecclesiastes 4:9–10 teaches us the wisdom of involving others: "Two are better than one. . . . For if they fall, one will lift up his fellow. But woe to him who is alone when he falls and has not another to lift him up!" There are immature friends who just let you vent and gossip, and then there are mature friends who listen well but also give you wise advice grounded in

God's word. Seek out these mature friends—the discerning ones—and share your struggles with them. "The purpose in a man's heart is like deep water, but a man of understanding will draw it out" (Prov. 20:5).

God-Given Leaders

It might seem strange to point you toward your church leaders when you're having problems with your church. There are certainly situations where leaders prove they can't be trusted and shouldn't be followed (Ezek. 34:1–24; Titus 1:10–16). But Scripture lays out a vision for church life where godly servant-leaders care for a group of believers who respect, trust, and follow them as God's assigned shepherds (Acts 20:28; Heb. 13:7; 1 Pet. 5:1–5).

Within this vision, God says, "Obey your leaders and submit to them, for they are keeping watch over your souls, as those who will have to give an account. Let them do this with joy and not with groaning, for that would be of no advantage to you" (Heb. 13:17). So let your spiritual leaders help you discern the next steps forward as you reengage with your church.

———

As we wrestle with our lack of desire to be at church, these are three basic ways we can ask for help: (1) study the word of God, (2) talk with discerning friends, and (3) share with our God-given leaders.

Up to this point, we've explored our hearts and reminded ourselves to seek help. Now it's time to talk about the church.

What Is the Church?

The New Testament uses three images for the church that emphasize our togetherness: a family of siblings, a body with parts, and a temple with stones. The church is "the household of God," "the body of Christ," and "a dwelling place for the Spirit," built with "living stones" (1 Cor. 12:12–27; Eph. 2:21–22; 4:15–16; 1 Tim. 3:15; 1 Pet. 2:5). The implications are obvious:

families live together, body parts work together, and temple stones fit together.

Some people use these truths to discount church attendance. "The church is a people, not a place," they say. "It's about *being* the church, not *going* to church." But instead of lowering the bar, these images actually highlight the beauty and benefit of gathering with our fellow believers.

God's people have always been marked, known, and renewed by regular, rhythmic, orderly gatherings (Heb. 10:24–25). A body that's never together is more like a prosthetics warehouse, and a family that never has any dinners or outings or reunions won't be a healthy or happy family, if any family at all. No temple stands firm when its quarried stones refuse to stick together.

Being together—in person—is that important.

Sure, you could listen to some Christian music and an online sermon once a week, but there won't be any face-to-face fellowship or personalized care or communal bread and wine symbolizing the body and blood of Jesus. You could read the Bible and pray on your own, but you won't hear the studied voice of your own shepherd teaching and comforting and correcting you. You could even attend another church for a while because yours has grown unsatisfying, but that's not treating your local church like much of a covenant community.

A Covenant Family

There's a secret ingredient in every healthy family, body, or temple: commitment among the parts. Healthy families stay close and stick together. Healthy body parts stay strong and move together. Sturdy buildings stay fitted and bonded together.

Covenants are made for the hard times, not the good times. In the good times, we don't seem to need covenants because we can get by and stick together on feelings alone. But covenant communities hold us up when we're faltering and pick us up when we've fallen. They encourage us when we're weary and wake us when we're sleepy. They draw us out of ourselves and call us to our commitments and responsibilities. They invite us back to the garden of Christian community, where we grow.

The Bible is filled with covenants—God's commitments to his people that create our commitments to him. The church exists because Jesus died on the cross to ransom and cleanse us with his blood, which sealed the "new covenant" (Heb. 8:1–10:24). Every genuine Christian participates in this covenant, which means our sins are forgiven through the death of Christ as our substitute, we receive a spiritual heart transplant so that we love God and serve others, and we become part of God's spiritual family with all its rights and privileges—and all its responsibilities.

As a sophomore, I became the intramural sports coordinator at my small Christian college. I organized leagues, ran sign-ups, scheduled games, refereed every sport, and problem-solved all over the place. I held a paper route as a teenager and mowed lawns in high school, but this was my first experience dealing with hundreds of people and dozens of relational and logistical challenges. I was often uncomfortable. But I really grew as I served other people. Why? I had a responsibility.

Without a concrete set of roles and commitments, our desires to grow usually become a compost pile of good intentions. There's a reason why would-be soldiers *enlist*, and would-be graduates *enroll*, and would-be couples get *engaged*. Commitment strengthens us by making us shoulder responsibilities toward other people—especially when we don't feel like it.[2]

In the Old Testament, Israel held sacred ceremonies to renew their covenant commitments. The church has its own covenant renewal ceremony, called Communion or the Lord's Supper. This meal together is our regular, rhythmic reminder that we have peace with God through Christ, and that he's coming again soon (1 Cor. 11:23–26). But the new covenant doesn't just reassure us that we're reconciled with God and each other; this ceremony also calls us back to our responsibilities. It's easy to slip into thinking that worship services are mainly for *me*. But they're actually sacred gatherings where God feeds us *all* with his grace and renews our devotion both to him and to each other.

You see, covenants involve you, but they're not all about you. Covenants are about *us*.

It's Not All about You

I get it. It can be hard. The worship team didn't pull their song selections from your personal playlist. The pastor didn't have the time and resources to craft a mesmerizing sermon with a team of presidential speechwriters. The membership may not have the perfect combination of older saints to mentor you, younger saints to energize you, mature saints to counsel you, hospitable saints to host you, and outgoing saints to pursue you.

But if your church believes the Bible and preaches the gospel and practices the ordinances and serves one another, then your church has saints, and those saints are your brothers and sisters, your fathers and mothers, your weary fellow pilgrims walking the same wilderness you are—away from Egypt, led by cloud and fire, with eyes set on the promised land (Ex. 13:21–22; Heb. 12:1–2).

This isn't a solo hike. It's a holy caravan.

You see, those people you wish would pursue you and care for you and reach out to you also need you to do the same *for them* (Gal. 6:9–10).

That pastor you wish were a better preacher is probably praying that you'd be a good listener (Mark 4:3–8, 14–20; James 1:22–25). Those gifted people whose love you need also need your unique offering of love (Eph. 4:15–16). Even those whose company you find dissatisfying or unhelpful or just plain awkward don't need your criticism but your gospel partnership (Phil. 4:2–3).

And you can't do any of those things if you're not *present*.

The Power of Presence

In the church I now pastor, my predecessor served faithfully for more than thirty years. Many people have told me different stories about his influence in their lives, but they're all saying essentially the same thing. Based on their stories, I already have a title for his biography: *You Were There.*

- "You were there when our daughter was born."
- "You did my grandpa's funeral."
- "You came over after our son committed suicide."
- "You baptized my wife and me."

- "You shared the gospel with my dad."
- "You performed our wedding."
- "You wept with us when the cancer came back."

"You were there" are three of the finest words a friend can hear: *You came. You helped. You showed up. You were there.*

Solomon tells us, "Better is a neighbor who is near than a brother who is far away" (Prov. 27:10). Jesus didn't just heal lepers— he "touched" them (Matt. 8:3). Paul ached to see his churches "face to face" (1 Thess. 2:17; 3:10). John longed for the same personal connection: "Though I have much to write to you, I would rather not use paper and ink. Instead I hope to come to you and talk face to face, so that our joy may be complete" (2 John 12; cf. 3 John 13–14).

In our digital, fractured, lonely societies, we desperately need to recover the power of presence.

What Kind of Presence?

We all know it's possible to be physically present but emotionally absent. Dad can be home but checked out. A friend can hear your words without listening to your heart. There are people we hope *don't* show up to the meeting, the party, or the reunion, because their presence just isn't helpful. So what kind of presence should we bring to church—beyond just being there?

Consistent Presence

Acorns don't become oaks overnight. They grow because they stay in the soil, stay in the sun, and soak up regular rain. Christians are the same way. We grow by staying in the soil of spiritual community, feeding on the nutrients of God's word, being renewed by the Spirit among us. Gathering together around the gospel—on Sundays or any other day—is a main way God grows us.

Plowing, sowing, watering, and weeding are never spectacular activities. Neither is a roomful of Christians on an average weekend or a weary weeknight. Yet full orchards and mature Christians rise and ripen from such wise repetition.

In the Christian life, repetition is vital. *Consistently* meeting, *consistently* sharing, *consistently* teaching, *consistently* hearing, *consistently* praying, *consistently* singing, *consistently* serving—these are secret weapons in our battle against sin, invisible ingredients in the recipe of Christian joy, subtle nutrients that nurture our spiritual health. Consistency is one of the most underrated weapons in our walk with God. Like an acorn buried in a field, consistency isn't impressive—until one day, it is.

Honest Presence

Consistency means showing up no matter how we feel. But many people struggle with going to church because they don't feel like they're being honest about what's going on in their lives. Sometimes they don't believe anyone else is being real either.

We're sometimes told to forget our struggles so we can focus in church, but actually, God calls us to do the opposite. Jesus says, "Come to me, all who labor and are heavy laden, and I will give you rest" (Matt. 11:28). God invites us to "cast all your anxieties on him, because he cares for you" (1 Pet. 5:7). David says to God, "You have . . . put my tears in your bottle" (Ps. 56:8). The psalms are filled with weary believers crying out to God—in public—for provision, protection, vindication, forgiveness, strength, hope, and rest. The gathered church should sound the same.

The best way to foster honesty at church is not to condemn everyone else for being fake. The best way to foster honesty is honesty. The first person to open up and share personally in a group often opens the floodgates so that others share more personally as well. Why not be that person at your church?

This doesn't mean we show up wallowing in self-pity or simmering with anger. Being "open" shouldn't mean venting, ranting, whining, or provoking people with unfiltered words and attitudes. But it does mean bringing our real selves to church and letting God's healing grace wash over our broken lives.

People won't always respond the way we want. They might say something trite, sit in awkward silence, or even talk about us later. But the gospel of grace frees us to lay down our camouflage and embrace the full cover of Christ's righteousness (2 Cor. 5:21).

When we meet together, better a sad face than a happy mask. Better a broken heart than a whole hypocrite. After all, one of the best public prayers in the Bible comes from a spiritual outcast crying for help: "God, be merciful to me, a sinner!" (Luke 18:13).

Humble Presence

When we're struggling to be at church, it's tempting to be self-centered. Sadness easily morphs into self-pity. Cynicism quickly rots into criticism. The wrong kind of "honest presence" can make us downright mean.

It's always easier to tear down than build up, but the question is whether you want to leave behind a brush pile or an orchard. You can spend your energy sniping or serving, griping about others or giving of yourself. But it's hard to do both.

The prophet Elijah once thought he was the only faithful believer left, but God reminded him there were more than he thought (1 Kings 19:9–18). The apostle Paul spent his adult life dealing with serious problems in churches he loved, but he always longed to build up instead of tear down (2 Cor. 13:10). Jesus often rebuked his twelve disciples, but he stayed with them and served them till the end—even the one who betrayed him (John 13:1–15).

There are legitimate reasons to leave a church—like when it abandons the gospel, habitually refuses to address sin, or stands behind immoral leaders. But often we turn our opinions into convictions and our preferences into principles. We make everything black and white, with no room for gray (Rom. 14:1–15:7). Intramural debates become intergalactic battles, and we start majoring on minors (Matt. 23:23–24).

It's easy to criticize our churches, and sometimes, there's lots to criticize. But still, the best presence we can bring to church is not a critical or condemning presence, but a humble presence eager to listen and love, serve and build. "Do not grumble against one another, brothers" (James 5:9).

Unified Presence

There's a story from *Aesop's Fables* about four oxen who lived in a field. A lion often prowled around, but whenever he attacked, the oxen stood back to back, facing all four directions, so the lion encountered only their horns. Then one day the oxen started arguing. They got so angry they each retreated to a separate corner of the field. The lion then attacked them one by one, and the oxen were quickly consumed.

The Bible doesn't hide the reality of conflict. Jacob and Esau fought (Gen. 25:23), Aaron and Miriam envied Moses (Numbers 12), Jesus's disciples argued (Mark 9:34), Paul and Barnabas split (Acts 15:39), and Euodia and Syntyche stopped working side by side and started going toe to toe (Phil. 4:2–3).

Pride tempts us to minimize our similarities and maximize our differences. We forget that we're more alike than we are different, that we have more in common than what separates us. So Paul urges Christians to "agree in the Lord" (Phil. 4:2). Fighting in the churches broke his heart, but true unity fired up his joy: "Complete my joy by being of the same mind, having the same love" (Phil. 2:2).

We should pray, labor, and sacrifice for unity. "Blessed are the peacemakers, for they shall be called sons of God" (Matt. 5:9). We're called to cultivate

> compassionate hearts, kindness, humil-
> ity, meekness, and patience, bearing with
> one another and, if one has a complaint
> against another, forgiving each other; as
> the Lord has forgiven you, so you also must
> forgive. And above all these put on love,
> which binds everything together in perfect
> harmony. (Col. 3:12–14)

Growing Christians learn to view many smaller disagreements like the apostle Paul did: "Let those of us who are mature think this way, and if in anything you think otherwise, God will reveal that also to you" (Phil. 3:15).

Discerning Presence

Humility and unity do not mean checking our brains at the door: "The simple believes everything, but the prudent gives thought to his steps" (Prov. 14:15). Yes, we shouldn't be constant critics (Prov. 27:15), but we also shouldn't be naïve sheep who can't tell turf from grass or a wolf from a shepherd (Acts 20:28–30). Grace shouldn't make us gullible.

The Jews in Berea "received the word with all eagerness, examining the Scriptures daily" to see if the fresh gospel message was true (Acts 17:11). Mature Christians have "powers of discernment trained by constant practice to distinguish good from evil" (Heb. 5:14). Faithful Christians often speak up and nudge each other back onto the right track (Prov. 27:6).

Paul rebuked Peter when Peter undermined the gospel of grace by enforcing legalistic standards on fellow Christians (Gal. 2:11–21). Timothy was told to address anger, immodesty, and gender issues in the church (1 Tim. 2:8–15). James warned churches about treating rich and poor visitors differently (James 2:1–7). Paul even warned the Galatians against a potential future version of himself—if he ever came preaching a different gospel, they should reject him (Gal. 1:8)! Every Christian must be ready to discern right from wrong, wise from foolish, biblical from unbiblical.

If you're struggling with problems in your church, your job isn't to exaggerate *or* minimize the issues. Instead, consider following this process:

1) Study Scripture (Ps. 1:2).
2) Pray for insight (James 1:5).
3) Consider all sides (Prov. 18:17).
4) Weigh the issues (Prov. 17:13).
5) Examine yourself (Matt. 7:3–5).
6) Seek wise counsel (Prov. 11:14).
7) Pray for everyone involved (Rom. 12:12).
8) Determine your responsibility (Prov. 26:17).
9) Prepare to be patient (1 Thess. 5:14).
10) Act in faith (Prov. 3:5–6).
11) Speak up with gentleness (2 Tim. 2:25).
12) Give it time (1 Cor. 13:4).
13) Hope for the best (1 Cor. 13:7).

Along the way, remember that every church has problems because every church has people. Jesus didn't die for saints; he died for sinners. Then he sent his Spirit to make those sinners saints over a lifetime. So in most situations, when we discern a problem in our church body, our approach should resemble our response to a common illness or injury: a fair diagnosis, an accurate remedy, and a patient, disciplined treatment. Rarely is the first solution to amputate ourselves from the body and demand a transplant.

Active Presence

Just like there are two ways to be at a parade—marching or watching—there are two ways to be at church—active or passive. You can be a consumer or a contributor, a spectator or a servant. But if you want to be happy at church, become a contributor. Discover the secret of Christlike joy: "It is more blessed to give than to receive" (Acts 20:35).

The gospel is great news because Christ is a great gift (Rom. 8:32). But God doesn't just make us receptacles for his generosity; he makes us givers whose lives channel his love, a love "poured into our hearts through the Holy Spirit who has been given to us" (Rom. 5:5). The love of Christ toward us becomes the love of Christ in us, and the love of Christ in us becomes the love of Christ through us. "Just as I have loved you, you also are to love one another" (John 13:34).

What does this active love look like? In a word: *encouragement*.

Spectators tend to have three approaches: enjoy, evaluate, or criticize. But in Hebrews, when God urges a group of persecuted Christians to meet regularly, he gives them a clear assignment: encourage each other in the faith.

> And let us consider how to stir up one another to love and good works, not neglecting to meet together, as is the habit of some, but encouraging one another, and all the more as you see the Day drawing near. (Heb. 10:24–25)

Notice that the opposite of *skipping* isn't *attending*. The author doesn't just tell us to come instead of staying home; he tells us to encourage each other instead of neglecting to meet. Attending is the assumption; encouraging is the assignment.

The soldier in the field, the athlete in the stadium, the chef in the kitchen, and the Christian at church—they're all where they're supposed to be. But mere presence isn't the ultimate goal. The soldier should fight, the athlete should compete, the chef should cook, and the Christian should encourage his spiritual family.

This encouragement will look different depending on the person. We're all called to "speak the truth in love," so conversations are essential (Eph. 4:15–16). But each Christian also has unique spiritual tools called "gifts" that help build up fellow believers (Rom. 12:3–8).

Some Christians act superior, assuming their gifts are more important. Other Christians act inferior, assuming theirs are less important. But Paul urges us not to idolize or minimize any body part, because the foot, hand, ear, and eye all play a vital role (1 Cor. 12:12–26). It's good that "we do not all have the same function" (Rom. 12:4).

How do you discover your gifts so that you can use them to serve your church? Look for needs, start serving, discover what you enjoy, listen to feedback, and stay focused on love. Pour your energy into serving others—like pouring love into a funnel—and God will channel your willing spirit in the right direction.

Imperfect Presence

Stay in the church long enough and you're sure to be disappointed—and you'll disappoint others. You'll experience conflict, division, gossip, pettiness, anger, apathy—the full range of human failure. You'll see it in young and old, leaders and followers, longtime members and brand-new guests. If you're humble, you'll especially see it in yourself: "Surely there is not a righteous man on earth who does good and never sins" (Eccles. 7:20).

This brokenness is nothing new. David committed adultery and murder (2 Samuel 11). James and John promoted themselves (Mark 10:37). Peter denied that he knew Jesus (Matt. 26:69–75). Even Barnabas, known for his welcoming spirit, stiff-armed other Christians (Gal. 2:11–14). The gathered church is not a warehouse of perfect prototypes but a workshop of saved sinners under construction.

Yet our shared defects in God's family are no reason to choose estrangement over fellowship. Instead of distance, we should respond with diligence: "admonish the idle, encourage the fainthearted, help the weak, be patient with them all" (1 Thess. 5:14). Don't stop showing up because your church is flawed or because you're flawed. Instead, show up and patiently participate in the lifelong restoration process. God promises every Christian and every church that "he who began a good work in you will bring it to completion" (Phil. 1:6).

Forgiving Presence

Shortly after I became a pastor, a longtime member scheduled a meeting with me. This person wanted to tell me all about our church. But what came out was only a cascade of frustrations. Later that night, I wrote down all the specific complaints I could remember from our two-hour meeting. There were thirty-three grievances from this person's decades at the church. This fellow Christian couldn't stand our church after many years of choosing grudges over grace.

The path to resentment is paved with unforgiveness. But Jesus teaches us a better way: We only flourish when we're forgiven and we forgive. No wonder he taught us to pray, "For-give us our debts, as we also have forgiven our debtors" (Matt. 6:12). Paul writes: "Let all bit-terness and wrath and anger and clamor and slander be put away from you, along with all malice. Be kind to one another, tenderhearted, forgiving one another, as God in Christ forgave you" (Eph. 4:31–32). Nothing will keep you from church like a demanding and unforgiving heart. And nothing will strengthen your resolve to meet with your church family like deep, happy, peaceful, reconciled relationships that warm and strengthen the soul.

Prepared Presence

When my kids were little, I coached some of their sports teams. Before practice or games, the kids never wanted to stretch. They just wanted to play. But when I play any sport with adult men, we all stretch. We know our bodies need it.

There are seasons in the Christian life when there's little need to stretch. We feel lean and lithe, always ready to talk and give and share and serve and host. Our souls are soft, agile, ready. We're like kids running out to play—no warmup needed.

But the Christian life, though joyful, is not a playground. It's a battleground. Our souls grow cold, our hearts divided, our minds distracted. Some relationships are rich, but others fracture and fray. There are times of great energy, but sometimes apathy rules the day. With all the bumps and bruises, through all the ups and downs, we can forget the taste of God's grace and lose sight of his purposes.

In these seasons, the church can become a burden instead of a blessing. But with the Word guiding us, the Spirit helping us, and our spiritual siblings encouraging us, we can rediscover the warm, nurturing grace of our local church gatherings. Even before we get there, we can take some simple steps to become glad participants in what God is doing.

- Sleep well (Ps. 127:2).
- Meditate on truth (Ps. 1:2).
- Ask for grace (Heb. 4:16).
- Pray for the church (Phil. 1:9).
- Come ready to encourage others (Heb. 10:24).

Rain in the Fields

At all times and in all places, the gathering of the saints is like fresh rain sent by God to strengthen his people. Christians gather to worship not because it *might* be helpful if all the stars align; or if our leaders plan the service just right; or if everyone smiles at us with the perfect degree of sincerity, handles the small talk seamlessly, and engages us with just the right depth of conversation.

We don't gather to be cool, because we're not. We don't gather because there are just enough people our age, because that's not the point. We don't gather because we're safe, because in many places around the world, we're not. We don't gather because it's easy or convenient, because we don't follow a Savior who carried a pillow but a cross.

Instead we gather because we're saved. We gather because we're forgiven. We gather because we're one. We gather because we're redeemed, reborn, and commissioned to take the gospel to the ends of the earth. We gather because the God we're worshiping has instituted our gathering as the main way he matures and trains and comforts us. It's not just when the songs or prayers or sermons touch our souls right where we need to be touched. We meet because God builds up his people through our meeting every time, in every place, without fail, no matter how we feel. Like rain in the fields, it's how our gatherings work.

A Personal Account

I've experienced chronic pain, financial stress, grad-school schedules, parenting struggles, physical exhaustion, ministry burdens, relational conflict, prolonged discouragement, and church splits. I've often felt like staying home on a Sunday, I've pulled up in the parking lot with a longing to be alone, I've drawn a deep breath before walking in the door, and I've sat in the congregation weary and overwhelmed. I've often wanted to stay in my own world instead of rejoining the community of faith for yet another gathering. But almost without fail, my spirit has been renewed by the songs and the scriptures, the prayers and the praise, the honesty and the laughter, the bread and the cup, and the sheer responsibility to get out of my own head and look after someone else.

I notice a guest, and I'm compelled to welcome them, regardless of my personality. A song begins, and while it's not my favorite, I notice a friend deeply engaged, and I'm thankful she's encouraged. I hear a testimony, and a burst of spiritual longing fills my heart as I resonate with God's work in someone else's life. My pastor starts preaching, and while he's no Athenian orator, he knows *us*, he's been praying for *us*, and he's prepared his message for *us*. He's *our* shepherd, assigned by Christ to this flock in this field for this season. I start hearing truth and feeling conviction and sensing courage and love in ways I never would on my own.

Communion begins, and I realize I've been keeping my sins to myself instead of resting them in the Lord's impaled hands. I look across the aisle and notice someone I had a conflict with a few years back. Bitterness starts simmering. Suddenly I'm distracted and frustrated. But it's hard to sing the next hymn without remembering my responsibility to repent for my part and forgive him for his. We close in prayer, and I'm still tired, but somehow refreshed. I'm not sure who I'll talk with as the service wraps up, but God guides me, and handshake after hug after "hello," our church family reunites.

These are my people, because these are God's people. Cameron has a new job—we prayed about that a month ago. Jackie has an upcoming surgery—may God have mercy. James is grateful for the sermon, and so am I. Amber brought a friend, and she's interested in coming back to hear more about the gospel, which has a power I'd forgotten.

The whole experience pulls me out of myself and draws my soul back to the gospel. I'm still walking on earth, but my mind and heart are drawn up to heaven where I'm already seated and secure with Christ (Eph. 2:6), who gave his life for me so that I might share his life forever. And this gift is not only for me; it's for *us*.

Ask for Grace and Go

I know you might not feel like it this weekend. You might not feel like it for a while. The reasons you don't feel like going to church might be good, bad, or ugly. But, as a fellow sheep loved by the same Shepherd, I'm asking you to trust God, ask for grace, and go.

Go, because the church gathers every Sunday to remember the death of Jesus for our sins and the resurrection of Christ from the dead, and that's precisely what we all need to remember and celebrate, regardless of what else is happening in our lives.

Go, because like Martha, you've been working all week, and like Mary, you need to sit at the feet of Jesus and hear his word (Luke 10:38–42).

Go, because the songs of the saints are the soundtrack of the Bible, and your soul needs to sing and hear singing more than you'll ever know.

Go, because the Bible you'll hear tells the true story of the world, and the gathering of heaven's saints on earth is nothing less than the presence of the future.

Go, because the gifts Christ poured into your life didn't come with a receipt, and you have the happy duty to use these God-given tools to build up his spiritual house.

Go, because even though your church has problems, your church also has a Savior, a healer, a shepherd, and a friend.

Go, because right there with you or somewhere far away, there's a brother or sister who's hurting or hungry or persecuted or imprisoned, and if your church family is worshiping, so can you.

Go, because the world's been seducing your senses all week, but what you most need to see, hear, taste, and touch are the waters of baptism and the body and blood of Christ.

Go, because the rest you ultimately need is not just sleeping in or getting out of town but rediscovering the gospel's promise that in Christ you're forgiven, new, and free.

Go, because the stone trapping you in the cave of anger or bitterness or despair or doubt or loneliness or fear can be rolled away in a night, and once God does it, no Roman soldier or Jewish priest can stop him.

Go, because the good news of this gospel is not just that *you're* reconciled to God but that *we're* reconciled to each other.

Go, not because your trials aren't real, but because that table with bread and wine represents the crucifixion of the worst sins you could ever commit and the worst realities you'll ever experience.

Go, and in your going, grow. Go, and in your going, serve. Go, and in your going, let God pick up the shards of your heart and piece together the kind of mosaic that only gets fully crafted when his saints stay committed to his long-term building project—when we speak the truth to one another in love (Eph. 4:15–16).

The most important time to be at church is when you don't feel like it. So please, brothers and sisters, *go*.

Notes

1. Portions of this booklet are taken from David "Gunner" Gundersen, "The Most Important Time to Go to Church," *The Gospel Coalition* (blog), March 1, 2018, https://www.thegospelcoalition.org/article/most-important-time-to-go-to-church/.
2. This and the previous paragraph are adapted from a post titled "Growing Up: Six Basic Steps toward Maturity," on my personal blog (DavidAGundersen.com), May 1, 2017.

Scripture Index

IX **9Marks**

Building Healthy Churches

9Marks exists to equip church leaders with a biblical
vision and practical resources for displaying God's glory
to the nations through healthy churches.

To that end, we want to see churches characterized
by these nine marks of health:

1. Expositional Preaching
2. Biblical Theology
3. A Biblical Understanding of the Gospel
4. A Biblical Understanding of Conversion
5. A Biblical Understanding of Evangelism
6. Biblical Church Membership
7. Biblical Church Discipline
8. Biblical Discipleship
9. Biblical Church Leadership

Find all our Crossway titles
and other resources at
www.9Marks.org

9Marks | **Church Questions**

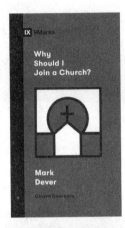

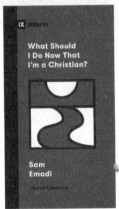

crossway.org